Hilda's Story: New Bedford, Massachusetts

Words By Siobhan McDonald

Pictures By Becky McDonald

Granger St. Studios

Ordering Information:
Quantity sales. Special discounts are available on quantity purchases by corporations, associations, and others.
For details, contact the publisher below.
Granger St. Studios ®
24 Birch St.
Marblehead, MA 01945
contactus@grangerstreetstudios.com
Visit us at www.grangerstreetstudios.com

ISBN 978-1-7330390-0-0

First Edition   Printed in the United States of America

For Hilda

For Mom
Because her love of reading
even surpasses her extraordinary love of stickers.
-SM

And to the woman who brought into this world
the most wonderful man I'll ever meet.
He is who he is, because of you!
-BM

Acknowledgements

With Grateful Thanks to:

My husband Dario Puerto — who sees the best version of me, even when I don't. Thanks for loving me (and feeding me) through this project...and always.

Becky McDonald — an incredibly talented and hard-working illustrator who also happens to be my fabulous sister-in-law (life does that sometimes).

The Residents of Windrose Woburn — who reminded me of the power of storytelling.

Kate Victory Hannisian — Editor extraordinaire, for your skill and enthusiasm.

DeAnn and Jill — for your support and encouragement.

Mr. Rogers — who welcomed me to his neighborhood, with love, long ago.

Tips on How to Use This Book

Introduce the Book to Your Conversation Partner(s)

Tell your partner that this book might connect to their own experiences. Explain that you will be asking questions throughout the story, and you'd like to hear their thoughts. You can also give a brief explanation about why you chose to read this book.

"This is the story of a woman who grew up in a city in Massachusetts. I chose it because some of you also grew up in a city," or *"This is a story about a young second-generation American girl who becomes a nurse."*

Build in Time For Your Partner to Respond

Each illustration is accompanied by two questions. Choose one or both of the questions to begin a conversation. Once you spark some discussion, you may find yourself coming up with additional questions. It's possible that you spend an entire reading session on one page of the story, and that's ok. **The important thing is that your partner has the opportunity to interact and share their story with you!**

Consider Using Direct Prompts for Partners with Verbal Limitations

You can also ask your Partner to "Point to the car" or other direct prompts, but let your knowledge of them inform your prompts. Respect your Partner by using gentle, open-ended, non-judgmental questions as much as possible. *"What were some of your hobbies growing up?"* invites more discussion than *"Did you ever collect stamps?"* Some questions do not invite additional discussion (*"What color is the lunchbox?"*) but they may be useful for assessment purposes. If your Partner is unable to answer correctly that day, you can move on by saying something like, *"Colors can be tricky-why don't you tell me about what kind of lunchbox you had."*

Watch Your Audience

Pay attention to your partner's body language and facial expressions. Be sensitive to signs of confusion or anxiety. You may need to choose another page or book, give your partner something to hold while reading (like a squishy ball), or limit the time of your reading session.

Have Fun!

This is the most important tip!

Be responsive and respectful, and you'll be amazed at the stories you'll hear in return!

Here is Hilda. And here is a room at an Assisted Living Facility.

Hilda has health issues. She needs nurses and other experienced staff to provide care and help keep her safe.

Hilda is happy she has her own room, but misses whispering with her sister at night.

That was a long time ago. Sometimes yesterday feels closer than today.

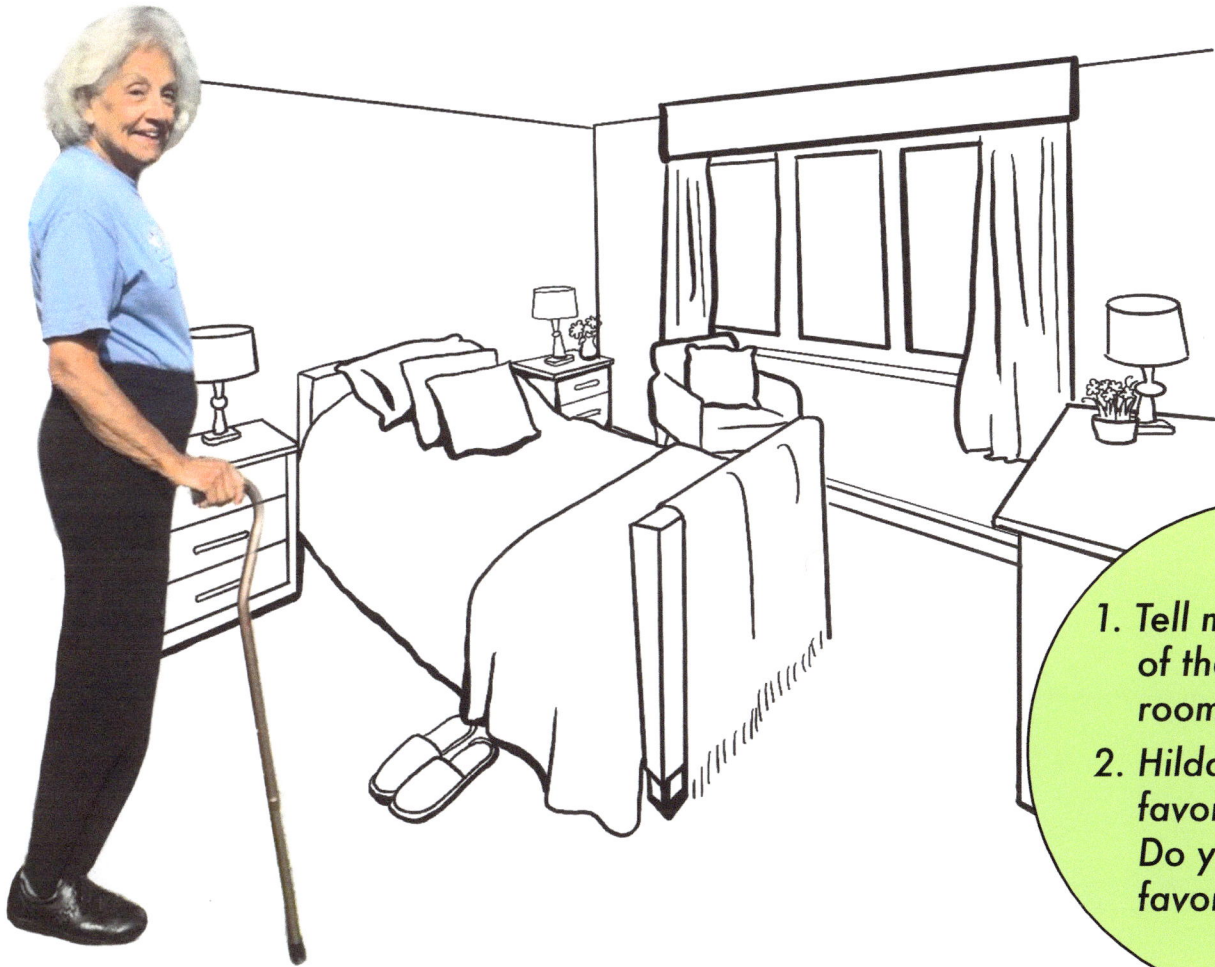

1. Tell me about some of the things in your room.
2. Hilda is wearing her favorite blue shirt. Do you have a favorite color?

1

Hilda grew up in New Bedford, Massachusetts, a city with a history of whaling, fishing, and textile mills. When Hilda was a little girl, she shared a room with her sister. At night, shadows made monsters on the walls, but the girls weren't afraid. They said their prayers and crawled into bed. They felt safe and warm snuggled beneath their cozy quilts.

1. Did you share a room when you were growing up?

2. Were you raised in a particular religion?

3

1. What's your favorite dessert?

2. What were family meals like at your house?

Sunday was church day.
After church, her family ate a
delicious Portuguese dinner.
Hilda's mom made the best rice pudding around.
Rice pudding is still Hilda's favorite dessert!

Mealtime was also time for sharing stories.
After they ate, they'd gather around the radio.
The Railroad Hour was one of their favorite programs.
They listened to musicals and comedies, and
sometimes Westerns, but never the news
when the children were around.

1. What kind of music do you like to listen to?

2. Did your family listen to the radio when you were growing up?

EXTRA NEW BEDFORD TIMES EXTRA

U.S. DECLARES WAR

d And Wounded
ack on Honolulu

1. Are you a veteran? Do you have a family member who was a veteran?

2. What big world events happened while you were growing up?

Hilda was mostly unaware of
World War II.
Parents often tried to protect their
children from the horror and
sadness of war.

Hilda was also protected from the outside world
at Our Lady of Mount Carmel School.
She walked to school with kids from the neighborhood
and enjoyed those friendships for many years.

1. Did you bring your lunch to school?

2. Tell me about your childhood friends.

1. What was your school like?

2. What did you like best about school?

Most of Hilda's teachers were nuns. They could be strict but she learned a lot. Hilda loved science, and was excited when they used microscopes. Everyone took turns looking through the black eyepieces. Things look very different when you see them up close.

Sometimes after school, Hilda helped her mom
with the baking. They made lots of different treats,
like Sweet Bread, Orange Cake, and Cinnamon Cookies
to share with family and friends.

1. Did you like baking? What did you like to make?

2. What were your favorite holiday foods?

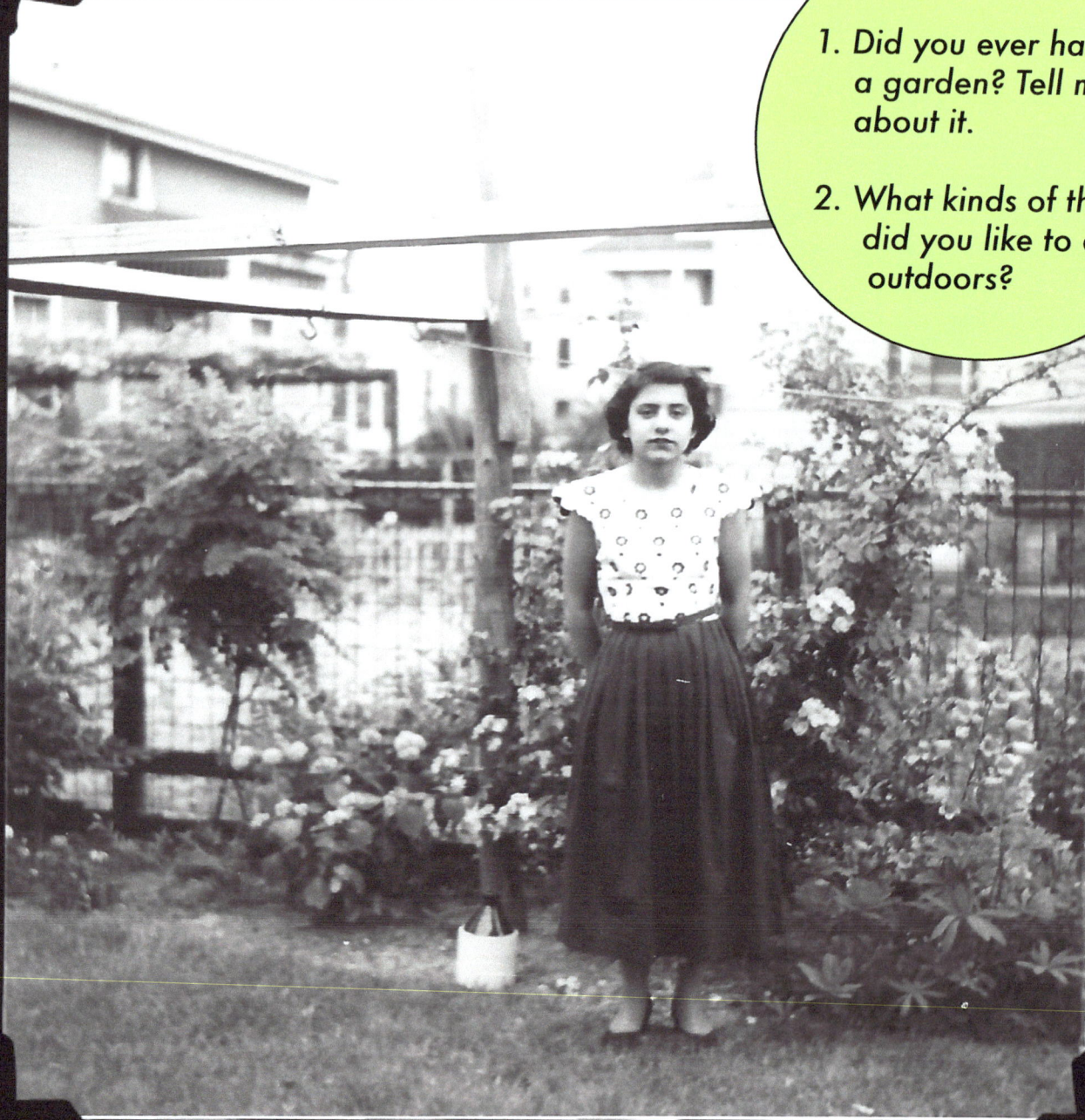

1. Did you ever have a garden? Tell me about it.

2. What kinds of things did you like to do outdoors?

16

She also helped her mom in the garden.
The edge of their driveway was lined with
delicate Tea Roses and Lily of the Valley.
They had a vegetable garden bursting with
tangy Beefsteak Tomatoes and colorful Bell Peppers.

When Hilda was a little older,
her family bought a television.
I Love Lucy made everybody laugh!

1. What did your family like to do for entertainment?

2. What new inventions do you most remember?

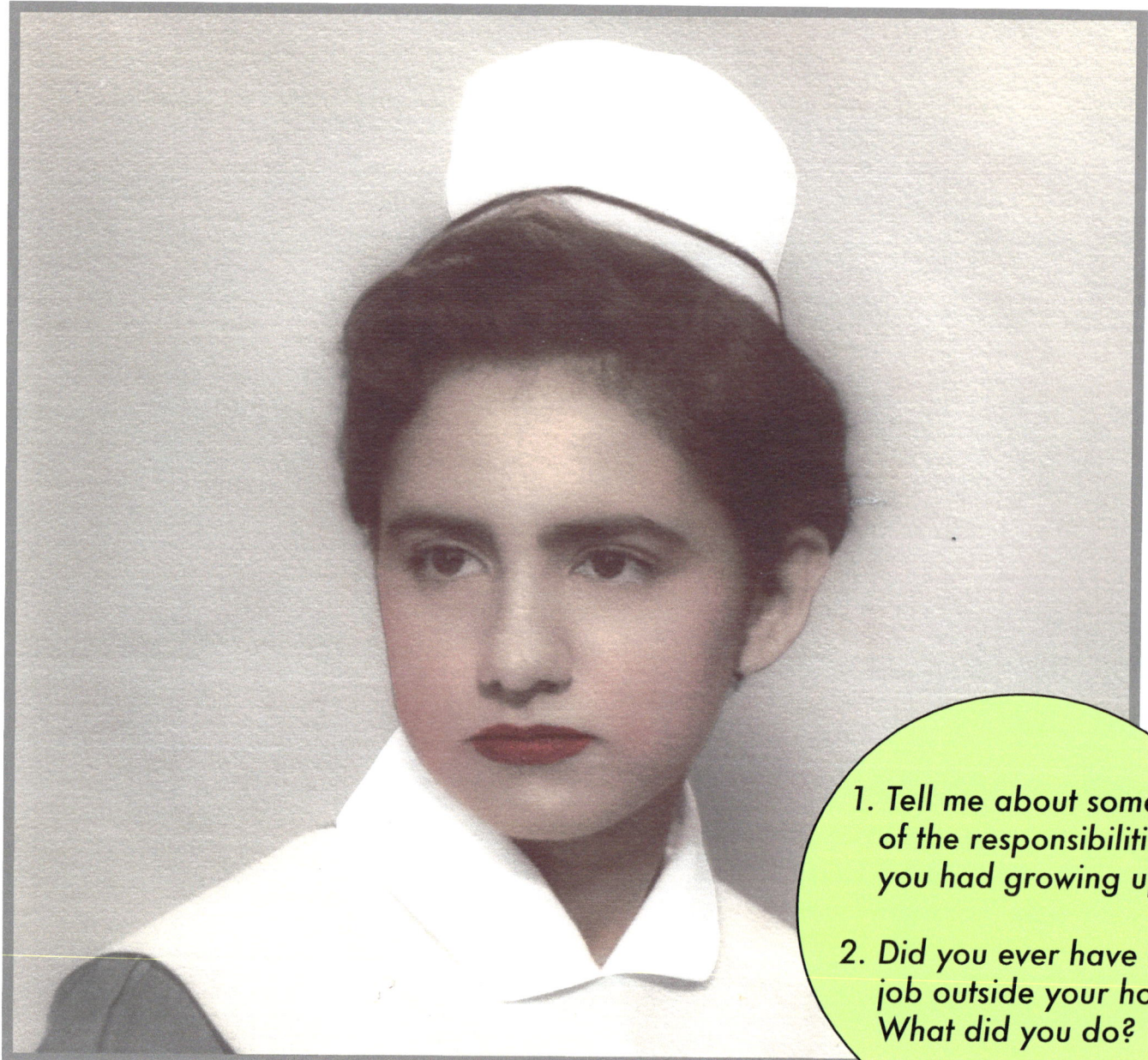

1. Tell me about some of the responsibilities you had growing up.

2. Did you ever have a job outside your home? What did you do?

Hilda graduated from Nursing School in 1957.
She helped a lot of people.
She was a nurse for over forty years.

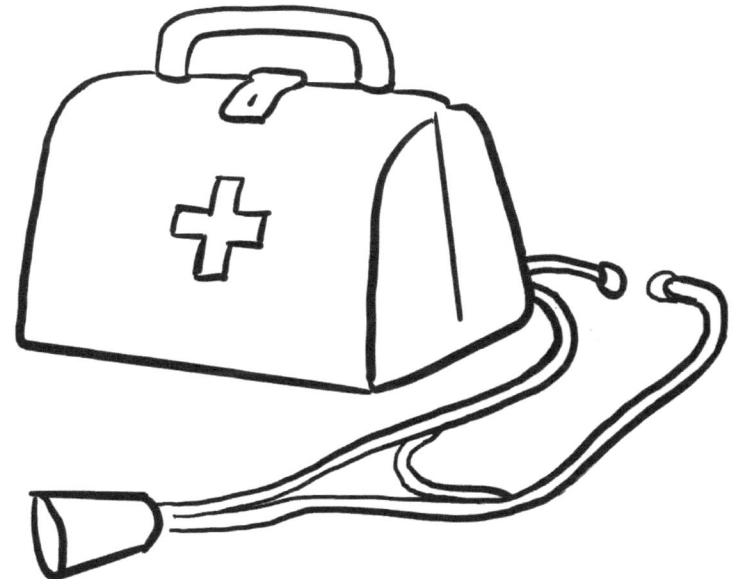

Some Friday nights, the nursing students
went to see a movie at the local cinema.
You could buy a box of popcorn for ten cents.
Hilda liked hers with extra butter!

1. What did you do for fun when you were a teenager?

2. What types of movies did you enjoy?

1. Did you have a favorite clothing store?

2. Tell me about the clothes you wore for a special occasion.

They also liked to go shopping.
New Bedford had lots of clothing
factories and lots of stores!
Hilda liked buying her dresses at the
Star Store. Back in the mid-1800s,
this huge department store sold
provisions and dry goods to whalers.

There were so many ways to have
fun growing up in the city.
New England winters were very cold, but
they went ice skating, sledding, and had
wonderful snowball fights!

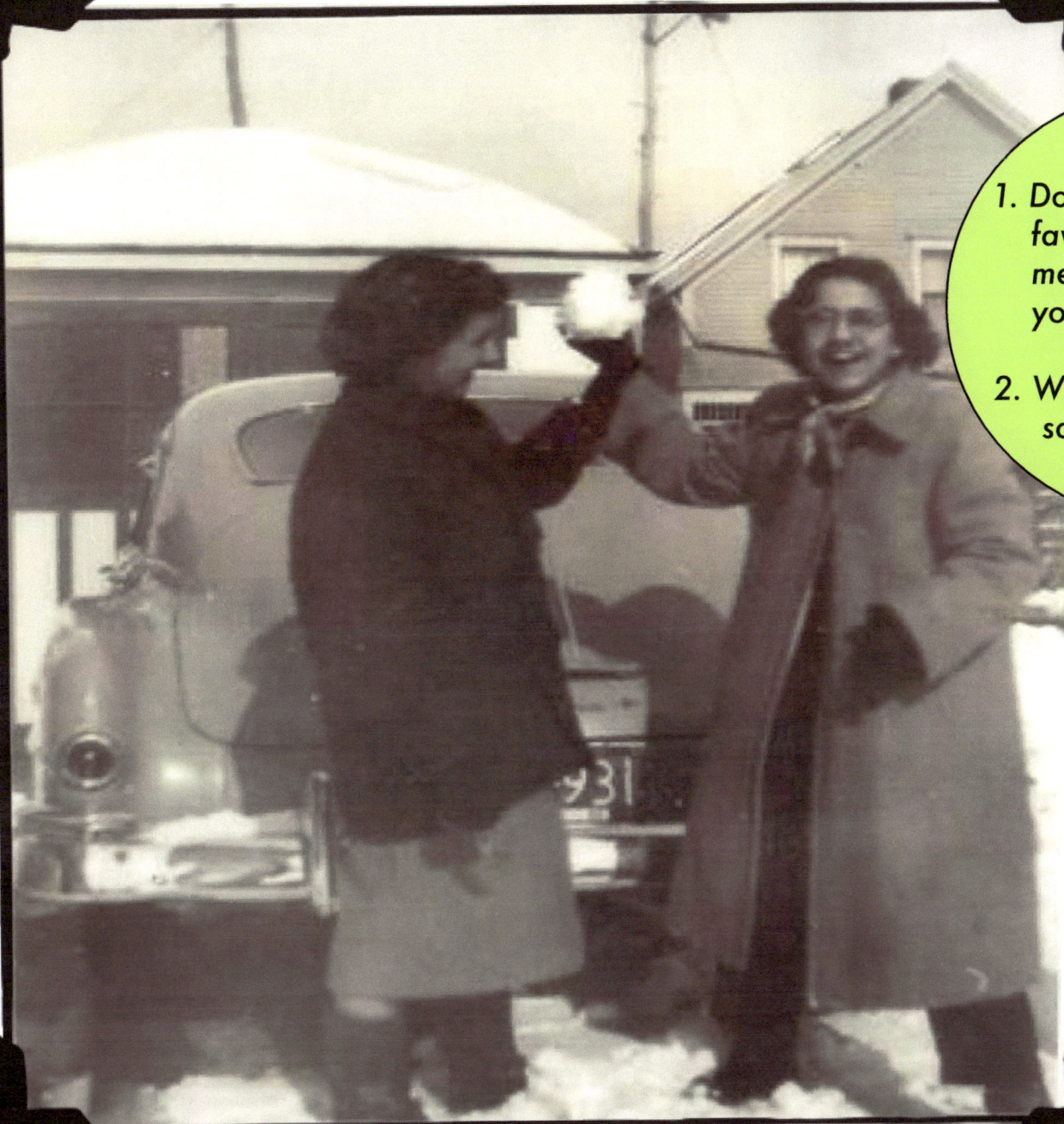

1. Do you have a favorite season? Tell me more about why it's your favorite.

2. What did you do on school holidays?

Hilda has had a lot of interesting
experiences in her life, and so have you!
Thanks for sharing some of your
stories with me!

Photo Licensing Info and Credits

About the Author

Siobhan McDonald uses her twenty-plus years of classroom experience to inform her business, Granger St. Studios. Providing visual arts workshops to seniors with memory challenges inspired this series of books. Siobhan is an artist, mother of two grown children, and "Vovó" (Grandma, in Portuguese). Her parents instilled in her both a love for reading and a need to use candles safely. Siobhan and her husband live in Massachusetts, land of delicious seafood, spectacular museums, breezy beaches, and history around every corner.

About the Illustrator

Becky McDonald has been drawing for half a century, and has written and illustrated dozens of personalized books under her product line, *Aunt Becky Books* (www.auntbeckybooks.com). When she's not visiting her three grown children in either New York City or Chicago, she's enjoying the quiet life with her husband and two cats in Western New York.

Share Your Story

We'd love to hear about how you shared this book with someone! Did reading together become part of your daily routine? What other questions occurred to you that may be helpful to other families and caregivers? Do you have a charming photo of an intergenerational story session you could share? We'd like to post these on our blog and create an ongoing resource of additional tips and questions to enrich the book.

You can also share your idea for a story. Please visit us at the Granger St. Studios website for sharing pics and ideas, and to keep informed about the latest happenings with our book series. Coming soon are several more books based on hobbies, travels, and nature. What interests you? We welcome your suggestions!

Share your story at
www.grangerstreetstudios.com

www.ingramcontent.com/pod-product-compliance
Lightning Source LLC
Chambersburg PA
CBHW040404100426

42811CB00017B/1828